D1531386

ʀeGENERATIONS
WHY CONNECTING GENERATIONS MATTERS
(and how to do it)

JESSICA STOLLINGS

ISBN: 1507760663
ISBN 13: 9781507760666
Library of Congress Control Number: 2015901649
CreateSpace Independent Publishing Platform
North Charleston, South Carolina

Dedicated to my Mom and Dad with heartfelt gratitude for teaching me what's important in life – and for always believing in me. It's an honor to further your legacy.

And to the five generations of family that have influenced my life, with respect for those who have come before and hope for those yet to come.

"Generations pass like the leaves fall from our family tree. Each season new life blossoms and grows, benefiting from the strength and experience of those who went before."

— HEIDI SWAPP

Table of Contents

INTRODUCTION

Why Generations Matter

E arly on in my research for *ReGenerations*, I asked my dad if he would sit down for a video interview about how growing up in the mid-20th century influenced the way he sees the world today. In his typical style, he was all in.

When he showed up at the studio in his best suit, my first reaction was to poke fun at him for dressing so formally. "Perfect Baby Boomer look, Dad," I said. "You even wore a tie!"

I didn't realize it right away, but my comments bothered him. His wardrobe choice was intentional, and the intention was not to come across as stiff. My dad wore a suit, he said, as a sign of respect for me and for the work I was doing.

Coming from a generation that often prefers flexibility over formality, I'd laughed at my dad's sincere effort to honor me. Ouch!

That mistake was a blow for me, a speaker who advocates cross-generational understanding and relationships. It also highlights how hard it can be for people of different generations to see past their own perspectives – and why it's important to be conscious of those differences to avoid misunderstandings.

Even after years of study and work on generational issues, I've found that there's no simple, mathematical solution. Human relationships are imperfect and unique, and they're influenced by a variety of factors – gender, religion, family, personality, ethnicity, socioeconomic background, temperament, personality, and education (to name just a few).

And while no set of criteria can fully define a person, understanding the significance of certain factors can shed light on that person's perspective. Knowing which generation a person comes from – and how it may impact his or her worldview – is an important piece of that puzzle.

In every sphere of life – with family, at work, in education, and in the community – you will meet people of different generations. Taking time to understand the generational factors that influence their attitudes, values, and perspectives will help you – and the organizations you're involved in – to be more successful.

Conflict among generations is nothing new; throughout human history it has been necessary for each generation to forge a path between the ways of the past and the challenges of the future. But in modern American society, the pace of change has increased so rapidly that it has simply outrun all of our past conventions.

Traditionally, older generations passed down stories, knowledge, and wisdom through oral tradition, often associated with family and community gatherings. Now families are scattered and living busy lives, and with the proliferation of technology over the last several decades, the world has become a vastly different place. Generations no longer interact in the same way.

For example, the technology-saturated generations of the 21st century send short messages back and forth on smartphones, an endless feedback loop of communication that can leave older generations frustrated by the lack of face-to-face interaction.

And then there's work. The past professional reality, where hard work over decades led to seniority and status, has been up-ended by a digital world where young people are sometimes catapulted by ability or opportunity into positions they never would have held before. Traditional chain-of-command structures are being flattened into malleable, ever-changing networks where authority is fluid and shared.

As a result, today's young workers often seek entrepreneurial avenues for success where a good idea – and the tech-savvy to translate it to the screen – can be all it takes to build a billion-dollar company.

As Baby Boomers retire from the workforce, employers are already seeing 20-somethings come to work with vastly different expectations. How can we maintain the knowledge, vision, and values of existing generations while allowing the fresh ideas and perspectives brought by new generations to make a positive mark?

The reality is that different generations still need each other – maybe now more than ever. We as a society need young, raw talent and the energy and potential that it brings. But we also need the wisdom and experiences of those who've lived more of life, who understand why a certain level of stability is needed to keep us all anchored.

Generations matter because each generation brings to the table a unique set of strengths that is important to our mutual success. Recognizing how different generations complement one another can help us move together into an increasingly positive future.

Jessica Stollings
Founder, ReGenerations

CHAPTER 1

American Generations: An Overview

Statistically speaking, generations are often classified by researchers based on their birth years. But more than just a demographic cohort, each generation has a distinct social or cultural identity that is influenced by large-scale trends and events during its members' formative years.

Practically speaking, it's helpful to our everyday interactions – in the home, the workplace, educational institutions, houses of worship, and communities – to have a basic understanding of these generational identities and how they influence people's attitudes and expectations.

Much like any other grouping of people in American society, a generation's worldview is influenced by a variety of factors – things like the economy, media messages, prevailing family structure, and major news events of their time.

As is true for people of different economic, geographic, or cultural backgrounds, groups of people who grow up in different eras often have different views about life and how the world should work.

The American Melting Pot

Imagine a group of strangers who've grown up in different parts of the country: a Wyoming cowboy and a New England academic, a West Coast socialite and an Appalachian farmer, a first-generation Texan and a Florida retiree, a family from the Mississippi Delta and one from suburban Ohio. Then put them in the same room together, and see how long it takes for a misunderstanding to occur.

In some cases, there may be a language barrier. But other differences arise from things as simple as the landscape: how can a Montana rancher explain wide open spaces to a man who's never left the concrete jungle of New York City? How can a description of the wooded paths that wind through the mountains of West Virginia make sense to someone raised in the hot New Mexico desert?

If you're in that room, it will help to understand the backgrounds of the people you're meeting with: their language, their landscape, their social and cultural influences, and how those things shape the way they see the world. These factors may explain why one person is worried about government interference while another calls for stronger policing – or why one is focused on the need for basic education and another on the pressure to meet fitness and fashion expectations.

And in our fast-changing American society, generational differences – the social and cultural differences that exist among people raised during different times in history – are every bit as distinct and as important in influencing how people interact with each other.

The Generational Melting Pot

Now imagine a group of strangers who've grown up in different times: a World War II veteran and a smartphone-addicted tech worker, a free-love hippie and a 1950s housewife, a middle-class factory worker from the 1970s and an unemployed boomerang kid from the 2010s. Put a family from the penny-pinching Great Depression in a room with one from the consumption-driven 1990s, and see how the conversation goes.

Pretend for a moment that it's possible to put all of them together in a room at the same age, say 27. How can the wartime vet explain the value of his childhood outdoor play to the tech-savvy software designer who grew up playing video games with his friends online? How can the father of two who picked from plentiful factory jobs and bought a house at 25 make sense of why his single, debt-plagued counterpart would move back in with his parents at 26?

If you're in this room, it will help to understand the generations of the people you're meeting with. This factor may help to explain why one person is worried about foreign policy while another is focused on neighborhood issues – or why one is focused on the need to keep taxes low and another on the need to alleviate the burden of student loans. Even at the same age, they have different priorities that reflect what's going on in their time period.

In just a few short decades, Americans have gone from horse-drawn carriages to men on the moon, from clunky telegraph wires that sent basic messages in dots and dashes to tiny personal computers that can send the history of human knowledge across the globe with the touch of a button.

As a result, social and cultural experiences vary from one American generation to the next in a way not experienced in most of human history.

Trends, Not Stereotypes

None of this is to say that members of a generation are all the same. Each person is uniquely made, and a wide variety of factors influence the people we turn out to be; there's no theory, tool, or test that can completely define who we are.

When researchers try to reduce people to stereotypes, it's referred to as "ethnographic dazzle" – a fancy word for being so enamored with surface differences that we miss important similarities.

ReGenerations does not seek to create labels or stereotypes, but rather to shed light on the idea of generation as an important social and cultural influence that shapes individuals. Not everyone necessarily fits into the generation defined by their birth year, but everyone does identify, to some extent, with the defining experiences of a generation.

Whether the difference is location (place), generation (time), or any other behavior influencer, understanding how and why people approach situations differently can be a great help in resolving conflicts and creating win-win situations.

The Study of Generations

Generational theory, which seeks to explain how the era in which a person was born affects his or her development and worldview, is a relatively new social science. Though it has early roots in the 1920s, it was not popularized as a field of study until the 1990s.

According to generational theory, our value systems are shaped during the early years of our lives by our families, friends, communities, and – in our ever-more interconnected world – media and defining national events.

In the 1920s and 1930s, the first serious generational scholar, Karl Mannheim, outlined the idea that each new generation experiences a gap between the ideals learned from older generations and the experienced realities of life.

As a result, a generational consciousness is formed out of "a common location in the historical dimension of the social process."[1] The resulting mentality and defining values continue to influence individuals throughout their lives.

For example, many of those who experienced the Great Depression – an era that was just beginning as Mannheim penned his essays – went on to be financially prudent throughout their lives. And many of those who served in World War II never lost the sense of duty that was necessary to defeat Hitler.

Baby Boomers who came of age in the postwar era of unprecedented opportunity naturally went on to value material success, while 20-somethings raised with the everyone-gets-a-trophy mindset of doting parents have struggled with a lasting sense of entitlement.

It's important to also note that generational differences are not the same as life stage differences, which change as a person ages. A teenager is in a different life stage than a parent of young children, who is in a different life stage from a person whose children are grown and on their own – and, unsurprisingly, a person's priorities, responsibilities, and outlook often shift as they move from one life stage to the next. Generational characteristics, however, remain constant throughout all stages of life.

Defining Social and Cultural Generations

In their book *Generations*, William Strauss and Neil Howe helped to popularize the idea that people in a particular age group tend to share a distinct set of beliefs, attitudes, values, and behaviors because they grow up and come of age during a particular period in history. They summed it up this way:

"History creates generations, and generations create history. The cycle draws forward energy from each generation's need to redefine the social role of each new phase of life it enters. And it draws circular energy from each generation's tendency to fill perceived gaps and to correct (indeed, overcorrect) the excesses of its elders."[2]

Strauss and Howe defined a "social generation" as the people born over roughly a 20-year span, about the length of one phase of life. More recently – particularly as the pace of technology development alters society on a much shorter timeline – researchers are looking at the possibility that, culturally, generational shifts are happening much faster, perhaps in half the time.

A Quick Glance at Today's Generations

Most researchers recognize six generational identities that represent the experiences of those born during the last century.

Generations at a Glance

BIRTH YEARS	ALSO CALLED	DEFINING MOMENTS	
GREATEST GENERATION			
1901-1924	"GI Generation"	• World War I	• Great Depression
TRADITIONALISTS			
1925-1945	"Silent Generation"	• Great Depression	• World War II
BABY BOOMERS			
1946-1964	"Boomers"	• JFK Assassination • Civil Rights • Vietnam • Hippies • Moon Landing	• Sexual Revolution • American Dream
GENERATION X			
1965-1981	"Baby Busters" "Gen-Xers"	• Challenger Disaster • Berlin Wall	• Divorce • MTV • Latchkey Kids
MILLENNIALS			
1982-2000	"Echo Boomers" "Generation Y"	• 9/11 Attacks • Y2K	• School Shootings • Social Media
iGEN			
2001-Present	"Homelanders" "Generation Z"	• Great Recession	• Terrorism • Technology

The major events that impact each generation occur when they are adolescents and young adults. This youthful period of their lives is often when their worldviews and opinions form and can be influenced by trends and events.

For example, Traditionalists were shaped by World War II because they were of military age during the war. Baby Boomers were influenced by the Vietnam War and the Civil Rights struggle because they were teens and young adults at the time. Gen-Xers were impacted by the rise in divorce because many of them saw their parents split up when they were kids. Millennials were influenced by fear of school shootings and terrorism because many such incidents occurred during their education years.

Since each generation is studied in roughly 20-year increments, it's not unusual that some defining moments span generations. Take, for example, the Great Depression. It shaped younger members of the Greatest Generation and older members of the Traditionalist generation.

This book will focus on the four generations that are front and center today: Traditionalists, Baby Boomers, Generation X, and Millennials.

As we get to know these generations, please keep in mind that one generation is not "better" or "worse" than another; one should not be glorified while another is ignored. Every generation has unique strengths and development areas, and they complement one another.

The 1930s were the golden age of radio. In that era, families gathered around their radios to hear news, sports, music, game shows, and dramatic stories.

CHAPTER 2

Meet the Traditionalists

1925–1945 | Roughly 75 million | About 10% of current workforce

The Traditionalist generation experienced a lot in their early years. They lived through the Great Depression and World War II, two events that would shape the 20th century on a global scale. Their collective experience – from economic privation to wartime rationing – is one of making do and stretching a little bit to go a long way.

Growing up, family and faith were paramount to the Traditionalist generation. Sunday church, followed by a big lunch and time with extended family (who often lived close by), was a savored weekly tradition.

Looking back on how little they had growing up and what great lives their parents provided for them despite relative poverty, Traditionalists sometimes have trouble understanding the more spendthrift and fast-paced ways of later generations who were raised in more prosperous times.

"When I was born, the United States was going through the Great Depression. My family was in a serious state of poverty. However, I never knew I was poor. I always had clothes. I never went to bed hungry. We always had plenty of food because my mother had a huge garden, and I think she planted everything but the kitchen sink!

What we did during my generation really helped lay the foundation for today's generation. I have that feeling because we paid the price. We made it. We survived in spite of all the handicaps; in spite of all the obstacles, we survived.

Things are too easy for the younger generation. They touch the button and don't have to think about it. We need to slow down and remember that Rome wasn't built in a day. Young people don't realize from whence it cometh."

– Jewel, born in 1929

About the Traditionalists

Traditionalists grew up in challenging times where loyalty to family and country and a self-sacrificing sense of duty were essential. Hard work and religious faith were important, and most members of this generation were raised in traditional nuclear families where men earned the income and women took care of the home and children. The Traditionalists are also known as "The Silent Generation" for their propensity to adhere to accepted standards.

Traditionalist Trends:

Their reality growing up: Hard times on the home front

Defining moments: Great Depression, World War II, Korean War

Where they went for information/entertainment: Radio

Their values: Loyalty, patriotism, duty before pleasure, faith, family, respect for authority, the common good

Who they admire: Presidents, generals

Their goal: Work hard and build a legacy (at work or in the home)

A typical "life path": Military service, early marriage and children, homemaking (women), working for a company for 30+ years and moving up over time (men), retirement with a pension, grandchildren

What they consider professional work attire: Suit and tie; skirt suit and hose for women (if and when women joined the workforce)

Communication style: Often modeled after the military chain of command. For example, "Here's what we're going to do; now, do it!"

Organizational style: Order, structure, and hierarchy

Strengths: Work ethic, loyalty, emotional maturity, stability, willingness to work together

Challenges: Reluctance to "buck the system" or make needed changes

In a word: Steady

Other things to know about Traditionalists:

- For the most part, they believe rules were made for a reason and should be followed rather than questioned.

- They like to partner with institutions for the greater good. For example, becoming involved in civic clubs was very common and respectable when they were younger, and the Traditionalists still comprise the bulk of membership in those clubs today.

- They tend to have conservative views of family, faith, and country.

- Their word is their bond. Traditionalists grew up in a time when handshakes were as legitimate as contracts.

Traditionalist Views On:

Work: Work is an opportunity, and hard work will bring rewards over time.

Church: Faith is foundational, and church should be attended every week.

Education: Education is a privilege.

Parenting: Children have a responsibility to help as part of the family, and they should generally be seen and not heard. Family togetherness and family meals are important.

Traditionalist Wisdom:

"Rome wasn't built in a day."

"Waste not, want not."

"Save for a rainy day."

Traditionalists

Military Service: A Social Obligation

When they were young, men of the Traditionalist generation served in the armed forces in greater numbers than any generation since, in large part because of World War II. Many still consider military service to be an important and honorable duty.

PERCENTAGE OF MALE VETERANS BY GENERATION [3]

24%	13%	6%	2%
TRADITIONALIST MEN	BABY BOOMER MEN	GENERATION X MEN	MILLENNIAL MEN

The Weekly Faithful

Traditionalists continue to attend church more than other generations. Many consider involvement in a faith community to be an important part of their participation in society.

PERCENTAGE OF EACH GENERATION WHO ATTENDED CHURCH WEEKLY IN 2014 [4]

TRADITIONALISTS	BABY BOOMERS	GEN X-ERS	MILLENNIALS
♂♂♂♂♂	♂♂♂♂	♂♂♂	♂♂♂
48% ATTENDED	37% ATTENDED	33% ATTENDED	30% ATTENDED

Life as a "Company Man"

Most Traditionalists have built successful careers through long-term employment, working 20 or more years for a single company. Younger generations, by contrast, have been accused of chronic job-hopping. According to Anya Kamenetz in *Fast Company*, the average length of time a person stays in his or her job is 4.4 years.

PERCENTAGE OF WORKERS AGE 35–64 IN THEIR CURRENT JOB FOR MORE THAN 10 YEARS [5]

1975 1980 1985 1990 1995 2000 2005 2010

51% >10 YEARS

39% >10 YEARS

When relating to Traditionalists, know that they often think:

- Faith, family, and country are important.

- Traditional values should be upheld.

- It takes time and hard work to build a legacy.

- Hierarchy and structure help to keep order.

- Authority should be respected.

- There is a clear distinction between right and wrong.

Tips to connect with a Traditionalist:

- Spend time with them, and ask about their lives and experiences.

- Respect authority and norms of courteous behavior.

- Use more formal communication in e-mail, such as proper capitalization and grammar.

- Be thoughtful about how you frame your "why" questions.

- Work hard and pay your dues.

- Help them capture their stories to share with emerging generations.

The 1960s were the heyday of television. When families across America gathered for their evening programs, they could see real and fictional events unfold on their TV screens.

CHAPTER 3

Meet the Baby Boomers

1946–1964 | Roughly 80 million | About 46% of current workforce

The Baby Boomers grew up in a time of economic prosperity and great change, and with the advent of television they were able to see national and world events unfold daily on the evening news. Their collective experience – from the Cold War to the tumultuous Civil Rights struggle – was one of shared fear and excitement, a sense that times were changing and that they were part of momentous historical events.

Looking back at the big changes that took place during their youth, such as improved racial equality, sweeping social programs, and the moon landing, they remember the sense of hope that enabled them to feel like they could shape their own destiny in the midst of change.

"I remember seeing the Beatles on television on the Ed Sullivan Show. They came in, played their guitars, and introduced a new style of music.

I also remember the excitement of hearing that we had actually landed on the moon.

Another early recollection is when John F. Kennedy was assassinated. There was great pain because so many people related to the enthusiasm of the youth, to the new vision that John F. Kennedy brought to the table. It was like it was a continuous thing: John. F. Kennedy being assassinated, the Civil Rights movement becoming more visible and the conflict growing, and Bobby Kennedy being assassinated, who many people thought would be the next President of the United States, and of Martin Luther King Jr., certainly one of the greatest leaders of our generation, being assassinated...and then we moved straight from that into the Vietnam War."

– Mike, born in 1957

About the Baby Boomers

Born during the spike in births that followed World War II, Baby Boomers grew up in a time of change on a national and global scale. Through events broadcast via television, they saw firsthand how individuals could make a positive difference in the midst of turmoil. When their sense of hope and possibility met the plentiful job opportunities of the booming postwar economy, the Baby Boomers found a path to economic prosperity.

Baby Boomer Trends:

Their reality growing up: Big changes in American society

Defining moments: Moon landing, civil rights, John F. Kennedy assassination, Vietnam War, Watergate, Woodstock, feminist movement, hippie movement

Where they went for information/entertainment: Television

Their values: Ambition, hard work, pursuit of "The American Dream," potential for an individual to change the world

Who they admire: Leaders of social and cultural change

Their goal: Pursue the American Dream and live the good life

A typical "life path": Follow a certain path of work and/or education and receive the corresponding measures of success, including a nice family and ownership of a nice home and car

What they consider professional work attire: Business suit; in some cases, slacks and a collared shirt (men) or a skirt and blouse (women)

Communication style: Professional, face-to-face, phone, e-mail, politically correct

Organizational style: Structure, hierarchy

Strengths: Work ethic, dedication, optimism, competitiveness, willingness to sacrifice to achieve success

Challenges: Difficulty with change

In a word: Ambition

Other things to know about Baby Boomers:

- As young people, Boomers questioned authority much more than Traditionalists, and they encouraged equality. In many cases, they were free-spirited hippies before they came to the boardroom.

- More educated than previous generations, they were highly competitive when they joined the workforce – there are so many of them that they had to be.

- They are creative and savvy. The Baby Boomers sent a man to the moon with minimal technology and organized the civil rights movement long before the existence of social media.

Baby Boomer Views On:

Work: Work hard, pay your dues, and move up the ladder. Dedication is a path to success.

Church: Faith is important, and you should take your family to church.

Education: Education is valuable and leads to greater possibilities for your future.

Parenting: You should treat your children as individuals and boost their self-esteem, and you should provide them with things that you didn't have growing up.

Baby Boomer Wisdom:

"Make love, not war."

"Don't trust anyone over 30."

"Civil disobedience works."

Baby Boomers

Raised in a booming postwar economy, the Baby Boomer generation joined the workforce with high ambitions. They were able to achieve an unprecedented standard of living, with many measures of financial success increasing substantially.

U.S. HOUSEHOLD INCOME

| $42,934 | $46,842 | $50,389 | $52,784 | $55,627 |
| 1967 | 1977 | 1987 | 1997 | 2007 |

Even adjusted for inflation, the median household income has risen steadily in the U.S. [6]

SIZE OF THE AMERICAN HOME

| 1,725 SQ FT | 2,095 SQ FT | 2,330 SQ FT | 2,598 SQ FT |
| 1983 | 1993 | 2003 | 2013 |

The average size of the American home has increased as Baby Boomers have increased their wealth. [7]

The Sandwich Generation

With the elderly living longer thanks to improved living standards and medical care, and young adults pursuing education and other goals before leaving the nest, many Baby Boomers have found themselves in a scenario less common among their predecessors: caring for two generations at once.

According to the Pew Research Center website, nearly half (47%) of adults in their 40s or 50s have a parent age 65 or older *and* are either raising a young child or financially supporting a grown child age 18 or older.

About one in seven middle-aged adults (15%) is providing financial support to *both* an aging parent and a child. [8]

Who is Dr. Spock?

Dr. Benjamin Spock was a pediatrician whose writing influenced a shift in parenting attitudes in America. For half a century, his book *Baby and Child Care* was the second-best-selling book next to the Bible. Dr. Spock advocated that parents be more affectionate with their children and treat them as individuals.

In more recent decades, the attitudes he promoted have been blamed for creating young people who are less ready to face the realities of adult life. Parents who follow Dr. Spock's ideas have been accused of "self-esteem parenting" and "helicopter parenting."

When relating to Baby Boomers, know that they often think:

- Faith and family are still important.

- If you work hard and do a good job, opportunities to progress should come; don't look for shortcuts.

- Having a structure and a plan is a good thing.

- Long hours are sometimes necessary – and may be viewed as a measure of your work ethic.

- People should be recognized for their accomplishments.

- A nice home and a nice car are signs of success.

Tips to connect with a Baby Boomer:

- Respect their experiences and recognize their contributions.

- Take time to build rapport.

- Say "thank you" and use courteous communication.

- Ask them to lead and mentor.

- Continue to provide them with opportunities for learning and development.

- Utilize their wisdom and knowledge, and help them to share it forward.

The 1990s saw the growth of the personal computer. Now it was possible for an individual to access a vast array of information and communication using the Internet.

CHAPTER 4

Meet Generation X

1965–1981 | Roughly 46 million | About 29% of current workforce

Generation X grew up with the fallout of many of the social changes that began during the Baby Boomers' time. Among them: scandals in government and religious institutions, large-scale corporate downsizing that came with globalization, and changes to prevailing work and family structures – including mothers in the workforce, after-school "latchkey" care, and a high rate of divorce. This experience has left them with a more independent and skeptical approach to life, work, and family.

Generation X remembers the end of the Cold War, tragedies and successes in the space program, Operation Desert Storm, and the advent of personal computers, as well as the start of some troubling trends: the AIDS epidemic, the rise of crack cocaine, drunk driving, tainted Halloween candy, and the faces of missing children on milk cartons.

"I'll never forget the Challenger [space shuttle] disaster because for most kids who were of the age when that happened, we were in school, and everyone was watching it on TV at school because there was a teacher going into space and that was a big deal.

The other big thing was the coming down of the Berlin Wall. All those years of knowing the Berlin Wall had been there, then all of a sudden it was just being torn down by people my age and younger, which was pretty amazing.

I remember when they were making movies about my generation, like Reality Bites *and that kind of thing. We were called the slacker generation, which is such a misnomer. That's not what Generation X is at all. Flexible was the word that I had in my mind, and I think that's because things changed so quickly in our generation.*

We've had to be flexible, and so it's made us question when things don't change."

– René, born in 1971

About Generation X

Gen-Xers grew up with an unprecedented pace of change, not only in the development of world-changing technologies but also with the breakdown of major institutions, including the family. Also known as "Baby Busters," they are largely the children of Baby Boomers who intentionally had fewer kids than their parents did. They were the first generation to experience 24-hour news coverage, personal computers, cable and satellite TV, video tapes, video games, fax machines, pagers, and cell phones.

Generation X Trends:

Their reality growing up: Change is constant in every aspect of life

Defining moments: Challenger disaster, Berlin Wall coming down, Operation Desert Storm, divorce, "latchkey kids," International Space Station, HIV/AIDS epidemic, personal computers

Where they went for information/entertainment: Television and early Internet

Their values: Flexibility, work-life balance, skepticism, independence

Who they admire: Successful outside-the-box thinkers

Their goal: Enjoy life with a balanced approach

A typical "life path": Navigate a world of constant change, where the social and family structures their parents relied upon no longer exist

What they consider professional work attire: Business casual

Communication style: Relaxed, casual, e-mail

Organizational style: Decentralized and results-driven

Strengths: Adaptable, independent, flexible, creative, tech-savvy, productive, open-minded, not afraid to ask "why," work-life balance

Challenges: Reluctant to trust

In a word: Balance

Other things to know about Generation X:

- Generation X, as a relatively small generation, sometimes feels left out and misunderstood.

- These independent, self-sufficient, skeptical individuals are also experts at sniffing out a marketing ploy; to them, transparency is important.

- They're the last generation that routinely used handwritten notes and letters to communicate.

Generation X Views On:

Work: Work smarter, not harder. Employees should not be micromanaged; they should be given tasks and judged by results. Work can be done anywhere.

Church: Faith is meaningful. The church as an institution should be questioned.

Education: Education is a great opportunity and should be pursued. However, you should beware of the "get a degree and then land your dream job" formula; it no longer works.

Parenting: You should provide opportunities for your kids in the form of various extracurricular activities, but also have family time. Safety is important, and screen time should be balanced with the real world.

Generation X Wisdom:

"The only constant is change."

"Strike a balance in life."

"Be skeptical first and build trust with time."

Generation X

'Til Divorce Do Us Part

Year	Rate
1960	25.8%
1970	32.3%
1980	49.7%

With big changes in the American family, divorce rates skyrocketed, leaving many Gen-Xers on changing and relatively unstable ground in their formative years. Between 1960 and 1980, the divorce rate nearly doubled. [9]

The College Track

Generation X is currently the most educated generation, though researchers say the generation after them, the Millennials, are on track to earn more degrees once they all finish college.

EDUCATION LEVELS THROUGH THE YEARS [10]

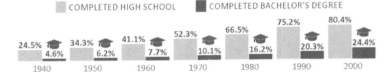

COMPLETED HIGH SCHOOL   COMPLETED BACHELOR'S DEGREE

	1940	1950	1960	1970	1980	1990	2000
Completed High School	24.5%	34.3%	41.1%	52.3%	66.5%	75.2%	80.4%
Completed Bachelor's Degree	4.6%	6.2%	7.7%	10.1%	16.2%	20.3%	24.4%

Seeking Work–Life Balance

With the large-scale corporate downsizing of the 1970s and 80s, members of Generation X saw the pain inflicted on their parents. People who'd bought into the promise of 30 years and a pension got burned – and Gen-Xers vowed never to be them, instead pursuing more independent and flexible routes.

Sylvia Ann Hewlett notes in the *Harvard Business Review* that 70% of Gen-Xers say they prefer to work independently. [11]

Research by Hewlett and Lauren Chivee highlights another trend where 37% of Gen-Xers have "one foot out the door" of their current jobs, and they are looking to leave their current employers within three years. [12]

When relating to Gen-Xers, know that they often think:

- Personal or family life comes first before work, church, clubs, and other commitments.

- You should be skeptical first, and trusting only when it's proven safe.

- It takes time to build trust, and transparency is the first step.

- It's important to ask and understand "why."

- Rules are just guidelines, and the status quo should be challenged.

- Balance and flexibility are key.

- You have to go with the flow.

Tips to connect with a Gen-Xer:

- Be open, honest, and transparent; know that it will take time to earn their trust.

- Promote work-life balance; reward with flexibility and mobility.

- Partner them with mentors they respect.

- Give them space; do not micromanage or give orders.

- Show respect for their time, be efficient, and use results-based language.

Bonus tip on relating to Gen-X: Embrace questions, and use them to help you improve.

For Generation X and the generations that follow, asking "Why?" is not necessarily about challenging authority. While older generations may consider it irritating or even insubordinate, more recent generations view it as an important way of learning how the world works.

Gen-Xers, who grew up in a time of social and economic upheaval – and, in many cases, the breakup of their families – have a different outlook on the world than past generations. That skepticism that always asks "Why?" is tied to a search for deeper understanding.

When Gen-Xers and Millennials ask "Why?" they're saying, "I care enough to ask" and "I'm interested" and "I want to know where I fit into the bigger picture so I can do a good job."

A willingness to embrace these questions and invite feedback is a way to create a workplace where people feel valued, appreciated, and part of a team working toward a meaningful goal.

The 2010s is the era of the smartphone. It's now possible to carry around a world of information, music, and video, and to communicate 24/7 via social media on a pocket-sized device.

CHAPTER 5

Meet the Millennials

1982–2000 | Roughly 76 million | About 15% of current workforce (but 30% of the population)

Millennials are the first generation who grew up with personal computers as a part of life. Older Millennials may have gotten their first computers in high school, while younger Millennials have had them in the home since birth. This has revolutionized how they communicate and how they see the world, viewing their connections through technology as another dimension of life.

In the instant-information age, Millennials are troubled by the violent trends of school shootings and terrorism that affect everyday people; their perception of the world is shaped by the horror of the 9/11 attacks. Despite the fears generated by these terrifying events, Millennials as a group have a sense of optimism and a strong desire to make a positive difference in the world.

"9/11 was a really big, distinct moment that I will never forget, along with the ridiculous amount of violence in this generation within schools. I feel like every six months something crazy, like the Batman movie [theatre shooting], happens, and it definitely gives people an idea that our generation is affected by video games or the Internet or the violence in movies and so we want to go out and do these things, and it gives our age group a bad name.

I think technology has made us really aware and passionate to see change, in that constantly you see a lot of people post on Facebook and different social media sites about injustices and violence and different things like that. Those things aren't really left under the radar anymore; people talk about them, and that's cool to see that people actually care about justice in this world right now.

Our generation can make a positive difference in violence, in areas like sex trafficking and modern-day slavery, and just so many different avenues of injustice that might not have been brought to light in years past just because of lack of information, lack of technology. To be able to have so many resources and outlets, I think it's spurring our generation to be more passionate and active about those things."

– Trevor, born in 1992

About Millennials

Millennials, also known as "Echo Boomers" or "Generation Y," grew up in a world with a whole new dimension: technology as a means to interact with and exchange information. This explosion of technology has meant exposure to a wide range of worldviews, ideas, and cultures; it has also given them access to world events in real time and has provided them an outlet to broadcast their thoughts as they happen. Technology has infiltrated every aspect of their lives, fundamentally changing the way this generation communicates and sees the world.

Millennial Trends:

Their reality growing up: Technology shapes the present and the future

Defining moments: 9/11 attacks, terrorism, Y2K, school shootings, reality TV, laptops, cell phones, online social networks

Where they went for information/entertainment: Internet

Their values: Creativity, collaboration, diversity, inclusion, authenticity, purpose, open-mindedness, entrepreneurialism, passion for global issues

Who they admire: Cause-oriented individuals and entrepreneurs

Their goal: Make a difference and change the world

A typical "life path": Pursue what they're passionate about and see where it leads; they are "dream job" chasers in search of their calling and ideal life

What they consider professional work attire: Anything that expresses their individual style

Communication style: Social media, texting, technology

Organizational style: Networked and relational; a team, not a hierarchy

Strengths: Tech-savvy, well-educated, high performing, networkers, confident, creative/entrepreneurial, optimistic, diverse, civic-minded, willing to work hard to make a positive difference

Challenges: Sense of entitlement, short attention span, dependent on parents

In a word: Passion

Other things to know about Millennials:

- They grew up multi-tasking – they studied on their way to soccer practice while eating a fast-food burger.

- Though they're very cause-oriented and will readily support specific efforts or companies, they don't like to be branded with a religious or political category.

- Raised by Baby Boomer and Generation X parents with a self-esteem focus, many of them are sheltered, protected, praised, and privileged, and grew up with a paralyzing number of choices.

- They've experienced a major focus on safety, both in terms of crime/terrorism fears and in terms of parental supervision and strict regulations on everything from cribs and car seats.

- Most of them are burdened with student loan debt, and many have trouble finding work; however, they've largely faced the Great Recession with optimism.

- Millennials are growing up later, getting married later, and rethinking traditional "rites of passage" like home ownership.

- Millennials, who often live alone, register higher rates of depression, anxiety, and loneliness than other generations.

- Only 13 percent of Millennials say their career goal involves climbing the corporate ladder to become a CEO or president; by contrast, two-thirds say their goal involves starting their own business.[13]

Millennial Views On:

Work: You should be able to leave the building early if your work is done. Actually, why report to a building when you could work from home?

Church: You should ask questions rather than accept religion on blind faith. Attending church isn't necessary to gain spiritual community; it's more important that you put your faith into action.

Education: You should pursue higher education, but be aware that a pricey college degree might not help you as much as you thought.

Parenting: Strive for the ideal by following natural and holistic trends and scouring the Internet for the best strategies, products, and activities.

Millennial Wisdom:

"Follow your passion."

"Make a difference every day."

"Express yourself."

Millennials

According to Pew Research, Millennials are the most racially diverse generation in American history. [14]

About 43 percent of Millennial adults are non-white; *National Vital Statistics Reports* notes that about half of American newborns today are non-white, and the U.S. Census Bureau projects that non-whites will make up a majority of the population around 2043. [15]

RACE AND ETHNICITY IN 2011 [16]

GENERATION	WHITE	HISPANIC	BLACK	ASIAN	OTHER
Traditionalists	79%	7%	9%	4%	1%
Baby Boomers	73%	10%	11%	4%	1%
Generation X	62%	18%	12%	6%	2%
Millennials	59%	20%	14%	5%	2%

The Online Universe

SOCIAL MEDIA USE BY GENERATION [17]

TRADITIONALISTS USING SOCIAL MEDIA — 50%

BABY BOOMERS USING SOCIAL MEDIA — 65%

GENERATION X-ERS USING SOCIAL MEDIA — 78%

MILLENNIALS USING SOCIAL MEDIA — 90%

For Millennials, social media have taken off in a big way as a communication tool, for everything from keeping in touch with friends and family to meeting professional contacts.

No Rush to the Altar

Millennials are getting married far less than past generations. Here's the percentage of Millennials who are married, compared with other generations when they were the same age (18-32) that Millennials are now. [18]

MARRIED **TRADITIONALISTS** IN 1960 — 65%

MARRIED **BABY BOOMERS** IN 1980 — 48%

MARRIED **GENERATION X-ERS** IN 1997 — 36%

MARRIED **MILLENNIALS** IN 2013 — 26%

The Unwed Baby Boom

According to the Centers for Disease Control and Prevention, 40.8 percent of all U.S. births are to unwed mothers. For Millennials, the figure is well over 50 percent. [19]

1975   1980   1985   1990   1995   2000   2005   2010   2015

18.4%   28.0%   33.2%   40.8%

(OVER 50% FOR MILLENNIALS)

When relating to Millennials, know what they often think:

- It's easier to relate to family, friends, mentors, and coaches than to a "boss" figure.

- It's best to work together as a team.

- You can work remotely via technology; flexibility is key.

- Marriage, religion, and all traditional institutions/organizations are questionable.

- Life should be lived purposefully and in pursuit of the "ideal."

Tips to connect with a Millennial:

- Communicate your expectations from the start and offer regular feedback.

- Build genuine relationships; get to know them as people.

- Be transparent and authentic, and create a safe place for questions and doubts.

- Connect with a cause.

- Allow them to be creative and entrepreneurial.

- Provide mentoring, coaching, and teamwork; help them identify their strengths and where they fit in the bigger picture.

- Make sure you use the right communication channels. (Hint: Don't call; they won't pick up. If you text, they'll be right there!)

Bonus tips on communicating with Millennials:

- Rather than creating new programs, communicate what you currently have that Millennials want. In other words, tell them "why" they should be interested in your organization. If you're not sure what those things are, try this exercise:

  Make a list of two columns.
  Column 1: Jot down the programs, policies, and initiatives that are going well for you.
  Column 2: Based on what you've learned about Millennials, make a list of what they are looking for in a job, church, extracurricular activity, etc.
  Circle the areas of commonality, and promote those opportunities first!

- Make your messages short and interactive with infographics, action words, and forward-looking phrases.

- Don't lecture. Instead, ask questions and foster a dialogue.

- Evaluate your visual presentation and consider that Millennials are more drawn to fonts that look handwritten, colors that are green and earthy, and videos that are raw and relaxed (think YouTube).

CHAPTER 6

Look Back and Look Forward

I n addition to the four generations that currently make up the bulk of the American workforce, there are two other generations that have an impact on American society: the generation that came before the Traditionalists, known as the Greatest Generation, and the generation that's coming after the Millennials, whose identity is still being formed and is currently known as iGen.

Despite its relatively small number of living members, the Greatest Generation continues to have a lasting impact on American society, both through the institutions its members founded and through its impact on the Traditionalists and Baby Boomers, who they helped to raise.

The newest generation is iGen, which is currently made up of kids middle-school age and below. Since they haven't yet reached adulthood, we don't know yet what attributes and values will most characterize iGen, but we can get an idea through research and futurist predictions.

A Word on the Greatest Generation (1901–1924)

The Greatest Generation is so named because it's the generation that won two world wars and laid the foundation for much of the infrastructure and many of the institutions that we have in America today. Also called the GI Generation because of their high rate of military service, the Greatest Generation is known for its members' strong sense of duty, patriotism, work ethic, and the common good.

Among the accomplishments of the Greatest Generation were programs that put people to work building bridges and other infrastructure; construction of modern schools, hospitals, and highways across the country; development of social safety-net programs; and founding of businesses and charities that grew to national prominence. Much of what they built is still in use today.

Some researchers of generational theory suggest that generations come in cycles, and that the generations living at any one time complement one another by providing a full set of the traits, strengths, and experiences needed by society.

Early predictions for iGen, the generation born at the start of the 21st century, show similarities between those young people and the generation of their great-great-grandparents, who were born at the start of the 20th century. It will be interesting to see if today's children grow up to be another Greatest Generation with a knack for building society and solving global issues.

A Word about iGen
(2001–present)

There's no formal consensus yet on the name for iGen, the generation born in the early years of the 21st century. Largely the children
of Generation X and Millennial parents, members of iGen have
been described as "Millennials on steroids."

They're incredibly diverse – the first generation in which the
majority is non-white – and they're extremely high-tech. They're
also the first generation being born primarily out of wedlock, with
a high percentage being raised by single parents or in other non-
traditional family arrangements.

Members of iGen are also referred to as "Homelanders," a reference to the security-conscious post-9/11 world of the early 21st
century; "Screeners," a reference to their seeming inseparability
from technology; and "Generation Z," an alphabetical progres-
sion from Generations X and Y that also references the zombie/
post-apocalyptic genre of entertainment in popular culture.

As the oldest members of iGen begin to reach adoles-
cence, researchers are beginning to pinpoint their generational
characteristics.

Early indications are that their communication style is root-
ed in technology, as touch-screen devices have been present
throughout their lives. They're socially conscious, and, in a digi-
tally linked world, they think globally. As children of the Great
Recession, they're showing early signs of responsibility and
resilience.

A Glimpse at the Future

To get a firsthand glimpse of iGen's perspective, ReGenerations held focus groups that generated a variety of interesting comments reflective of the world as they see it. Here's a sampling:

"The world is wide open to us. It is so easy to access information and ideas." – Olivia, born 2002

"Everything is so polarized in America. If you speak, you will offend someone. Is there a balance?" – Kolten, born 2000

"We have so much information now – about how to care for the environment, for example. It's frustrating when things don't change." – Vijay, born 2002

In light of what we know about iGen so far, futurists have made some predictions. Compared with previous generations, they believe iGen will:

- Communicate more via technology than face-to-face

- Connect with people from around the world

- Be socially liberal and expect fairness and equality

- Travel less for work

- Be used to living with less and more responsible with what they have

- Not be bound by geography, ideology, etc.

For Better or Worse

Throughout the 20th century, people lived according to the belief that their children's generation would ultimately be better off financially than they were, and this largely proved true. Looking ahead at iGen, the expectations are split, with people generally more optimistic about their own children's future than that of iGen as a whole. According to Andrew Kohut for the Pew Research Center, 34% say the next generation will be financially as good or better off than their parents, while 61% say their own children will be financially as good or better off than their parents.[20]

CHAPTER 7

Find Your Fit

By now you probably have a pretty good idea which generation you belong to, based on your birth year or the social and cultural events you remember. It's also possible that you were born "on the cusp" between two generations – meaning that, because of where you fall on the time-cultural continuum, you could identify with characteristics of two generations. The same rules for interaction apply: understand your own generational outlook and make an effort to understand other perspectives.

If you're looking for help to determine which generation you belong to – or if you're a rare-but-true "cusper" – go online! The Internet offers a variety of quizzes to help you find your generational identity.

Can you remind me again why all this matters?

Great question! You want to learn about generations to help strengthen your relationships, both personally and within organizations. By understanding other generational perspectives – and how they relate to your own – you can interact with greater understanding and ultimately better results.

In the next four chapters, we'll take a look at some *generational translations.* We'll tackle four big ideas, explained with the help of real-life examples, which can help you learn how to communicate more effectively and to work more fruitfully with other generations

What is "Generational Translation"?

The phrase "lost in generational translation" refers to a moment when members of two different generations, both meaning well, fail to communicate because they are unaware of different generational perspectives. Here are a couple of examples:

- A Millennial sends an e-mail to his Traditionalist boss in typical informal style; the boss is frustrated because he perceives the lack of punctuation and capitalization as signs of disrespect.

- A college creates a formal mentoring program only to see it go unused; students feel they can get the mentoring advice they need informally, over a few coffee dates scheduled independent of the program.

This kind of generational disconnect is something that can be avoided through better education and awareness. It's important to approach generational issues with an open mind about other perspectives, seeking to understand first and to be understood second.

The goal is not for anyone to be "right" or "wrong," but to understand one another and reach creative resolutions that result in a smoother-functioning workplace or organization – one that gets better and stronger with time.

How do I translate among generations?

Regardless of which generation you belong to and which generation (or generations) you're seeking to reach with your communication, the thought process for effective communication is the same:

1. Understand your own generational perspective

2. Understand other generational perspectives

3. Use this knowledge to better handle your interactions

Where do I start?

Begin with some self-reflection on how your generational perspective influences the way you see the world. Pause and consider how your experiences impact your responses and reactions.

For example, ask yourself:

- Where did I form my ideas about workplace arrival times, etiquette, and attire?
- How did I learn to write an e-mail, and why do I do it that way?
- Why do I feel irritated when I am questioned – or – Why do I always feel the need to ask questions?
- Why don't I receive feedback – or – Why am I always being pestered for feedback?
- Am I taking the time to listen and understand?
- If our perspectives differ, how can we work together in a way that gets the job done while respecting all points of view?

Once you understand your own perspective, take the time to understand others. Start by listening, asking questions before assuming, and putting yourself in the other person's shoes. Identifying areas you have in common also helps to break the ice and create a foundation you can build upon.

In the next four chapters, we'll look at examples of times when differing generational perceptions got in the way of communication – and what you can do to avoid situations like these. Before we get started, here's a "cheat sheet" of the generations that are front and center today:

Generation Overviews

	TRADITIONALISTS	BABY BOOMERS	GENERATION X	MILLENNIALS
BIRTH YEARS	1925-1945	1946-1964	1965-1981	1982-2000
A.K.A.	"Silent Generation"	"Boomers"	"Baby Busters" "Gen-Xers"	"Echo Boomers" "Generation Y"
DEFINING MOMENTS	• Great Depression • WWII	• JFK Assassination • Civil Rights • Vietnam • Sexual Revolution • Moon Landing • Watergate • Woodstock	• Challenger Disaster • MTV • "Latchkey Kids" • Berlin Wall • Divorce • Space Station • Operation Desert Storm	• 9/11 Attacks • Y2K • School Shootings • Reality TV • Technology • Social Media
CHARACTERISTICS	• Loyal • Patriotic • Duty before pleasure • Respect authority • Build a legacy	• Hard-working • Dedicated • Ambitious • Optimistic • Competitive • Sacrifice for success	• Independent • Skeptical • Balanced • Flexible • Mobile • Life, then work • Ask "why?"	• Tech-savvy • Multi-taskers • Well-educated • Collaborative • Creative • Passionate • Global
CONNECTION POINTS	• Ask about their lives • Respect authority and norms of courteous behavior • Work hard and pay your dues	• Respect their experiences • Recognize their contributions • Take time to build rapport • Utilize their knowledge	• Embrace their questions • Earn their trust • Be open, honest, and transparent • Promote life-work balance	• Communicate expectations from the start • Offer feedback • Provide mentoring, coaching, and teamwork

CHAPTER 8

Break Down Generational Walls

A lesson I learned from a "cubicle fort"

I couldn't have asked for a more classic generational conflict than the one experienced by my very first client. The company had two employees working side by side – a Baby Boomer and a Millennial – who were driving each other mad.

Each day, the Boomer came early and stayed late. She refrained from checking personal messages during working hours and always prepared in advance for the next day's work. The Millennial, by contrast, rolled into the office around 8:00-ish and packed up to leave before 5:00. She texted constantly, checked Facebook between meetings, and handled any evening work issues from home.

The Boomer felt like the Millennial was lazy, uncommitted, and disrespectful of company time; the Millennial, meanwhile, couldn't understand why her colleague was so uptight. When their frustration peaked, they came up with a solution. The company added a wall – a real physical barrier – between their desks.

A little bit of investigation revealed that the two employees had similar productivity levels and their customers were pleased with their service. They both produced high-quality work; they just did it in very different ways.

Helping the company to work through this conflict resulted in a new understanding between the two "cubicle fort" employees. It also revealed that expectations had never been set for how work would be handled or what would constitute proper use of company time. As a result, they brought a cross-generational team together to develop a policy that would help to avoid future conflicts.

The Bottom Line: Cross-generational conflicts in the workplace can lead to wall-building.

The Solution: Although "walls" – literal or figurative – may help us to tolerate one another in the short term, the real solution is to work together toward better understanding. Here are some ideas for how to help remove generational barriers within your organization.

Provide education about generations

Consider hosting a speaker, training session, or education series about generations. Focus on the unique identity of each generation, and allow members of each generation to teach their segment in a fun and creative way. Sharing stories, experiences, and lessons learned is always a great way to get the conversation started.

Here are some things tried successfully by clients:

- A church group hosted a cross-generational panel discussion on life, relationships, and faith across the generations.

It was fascinating to see how many different views emerged from the different times and circumstances in which the panel contributors grew up. For example, a snippet on "dating":

> Traditionalist: "Do you mean courting? My dad was very involved in the process."
> Millennial: "Guys text me some, but I've never actually been asked on a date."

- In conjunction with a speaking and training event, a company hosted a learning and development conference called "Looking Back, Moving Forward," with music from every decade and where participants dressed in the iconic fashion of their day and showcased the technology they used early in their careers.

- A middle school asked students to interview and report on different generations within their families. The students were amazed to learn that their grandparents got married young, used party-line telephones, and organized major social movements without Twitter.

Advocate for cross-generational relationships

- Spend intentional time with family members (holidays are a great time to do this) by asking about their lives and experiences. It's your legacy you're learning about, too!

- Mix up your church ministries. For example, you might pair a youth group and a seniors group for activities or service projects.

- Organize cross-generational project teams to solve complex problems. An interesting starting discussion would be: "How could our company best reward employees for their contributions?"

- Include a variety of ages on your boards, leadership teams, and committees. Expect a learning curve for younger members, and treat mistakes along the way as opportunities for coaching and mentoring.

Put your generational knowledge into action

- Be willing to put on different generational lenses to see the meaning behind different ways of doing things. The Boomer may be coming in early because she's competitive and links sacrifice with success; the Millennial may be texting all the time because it's her primary channel of communication, for business contacts as well as family and friends.

- When someone says or does something that irritates you, pause and ask yourself why. Could there be a generational difference at play? Think this through before you respond.

- Once you understand some of the attitudes, values, and perspectives of other generations, adapt your style to meet them where they are. Whether that means adding "yes, sir" to a verbal response or texting your employee instead of calling her, you may be surprised at how far a small step of respect can go.

- Be willing to think outside the box. My client's experience with the "cubicle fort" is evidence that people with very different generational styles can be equally good, productive employees. Can you offer the kind of flexibility in your organization that allows everyone to perform at their best?

CHAPTER 9

Communicate Expectations

A lesson I learned from an offending hat

A recent training session with the leadership of a church camp resulted in a major breakthrough between two camp leaders, a Traditionalist and a Millennial.

Near the start of the summer, as the Traditionalist led the campers in the blessing of a meal, the Millennial made a mistake: he kept his hat on, an action the Traditionalist took as a major sign of irreverence to God.

In front of everyone, the older leader had scolded the younger, humiliating him in front of his peers and the campers.

As it turned out, the younger man had meant no disrespect; he'd simply never been taught that a man was expected to remove his hat during a prayer. In our meeting, the Traditionalist wound up offering him one of the most genuine and heartfelt apologies I've heard. He'd assumed that the custom was universally known and hadn't realized his younger colleague was unaware. Then, the

Millennial broke down in tears. In addition to the hurt the incident had caused him, it had exposed a deeper insecurity: he wore the hat to hide the fact that he was losing his hair.

Once they talked through it, the Traditionalist resolved to try to avoid assumptions that would shame his colleague for things he may not know. The Millennial resolved to make an effort to show respect in ways that were important to the Traditionalist, even if he didn't always understand why. Healing occurred in the room that day, and it was powerful to watch.

The Bottom Line: Misunderstandings can result from differences between generations.

The Solution: Don't expect others to know what you're thinking, even if it seems obvious! Here are some ideas for how to avoid miscommunication from lack of knowledge.

Communicate workplace norms clearly

If your workplace has specific expectations, make sure you share them early on. For example:

- What time should employees show up?

- Do you have a dress code? If so, what is it?

- Can employees text during office hours?

- Can employees work from home?

Use an "onboarding" process

Whether you are an established or emerging leader, spend time up front setting clear expectations and then checking in with the new member of the organization periodically to see how things are going. Think of "onboarding" – the process of bringing a new employee on board – less as a one-day orientation and more as a weeks-long process of assimilation. This is also a great way to transfer your mission, vision, and values forward.

Review workplace norms for relevance

As the world continues to change, it's worth pausing to consider what's going well and what can be improved within your organization. Which traditions, policies, and practices are driving value and should be continued? Which ones have been continued merely because they're comfortable? For example:

- Does it make sense to ban texting when it's a good way for employees to reach clients?

- Are you spending money on travel for meetings that could be handled by videoconference?

- Are you losing potential new talent by requiring suits and ties?

- Will allowing established employees to telecommute save you space and money?

- Would a flexible schedule be as effective for some employees as working 8 to 5?

This kind of review is also a perfect opportunity to build understanding by bringing together a cross-generational team to work on the answers. It takes courage to work through these questions and make necessary changes, but in the long run your employees – and your bottom line – will thank you. Be brave!

CHAPTER 10

Change the Channel

A lesson I learned from an e-mailing professor

Midway through the semester, a university professor came to me very upset about her students. She had e-mailed them a homework assignment, and only one of the eight students had completed it. She wasn't sure what to do.

We looked into the situation and learned that most of the students didn't know about the assignment. Why? The professor had sent it by e-mail, while the students used Facebook messaging for their classes.

Yes, all of the students had been issued e-mail accounts by the university, but many of them had never logged in. Because they considered e-mail slow and outdated, they had instead opted for newer forms of communication like Facebook and text messaging.

Once the professor learned how her students communicated – and the students learned how their professor sent out her assignments – everyone was able to get on the same page.

After that, the students knew to check their university-issued e-mail accounts for assignments, and the professor learned that creating an account on Facebook would prove useful for collaborative discussions and project management.

The Bottom Line: Different generations often use different communication channels.

The Solution: Find out which communication channels your students or employees use for information, and establish clearly which channels they're expected to monitor. If the people you're trying to reach use different channels, consider adapting your message to the format they're used to.

Make sure your message is received

What's the best way (e-mail? text? phone?) to get in touch with your employee, family member, or youth group? To find out, ask them! If needed, adapt your style to use the platform they're familiar with. That might mean you text updates to the youth group, even though you still make a weekly phone call to your mother.

Stay balanced, keep an open mind, and don't expect one generation to suffer a major inconvenience to accommodate another. Each generation must be willing to adapt and collaborate, but it's your responsibility as the sender of the message to communicate your information in ways that will be received.

In addition to a channel for official messages, it's also important to have a channel where ongoing communication can occur. Be sure to choose a relevant channel for collaboration – whether that's e-mail, group text messaging, or social media – and make it clear from the start that everyone is expected to monitor and use this channel to stay in the communication loop.

Consider this generational communication cheat sheet when relating to different generations

When communicating with Traditionalists and Boomers, remember to:

- Listen first, talk second.

- Use proper grammar and punctuation in written communications.

- Use courteous phrases like "Please" and "Thank you."

- Use respectful phrasing when asking "why" by first sharing your intent.

When communicating with Gen-Xers and Millennials, remember to:

- Be open, honest, and transparent.

- Share "why" you are suggesting that they do something.

- Remain open for questions and two-way dialogue.

- Keep your messages short, visual, and to the point. Infographics are a great way to do this!

Communicate in a way that all generations can hear

- Use stories; this medium unites us all as humans.

- Ask questions; they allow each person to relate the issue to his or her personal experience.

- Use multi-generational faces in your advertising.

- Use a variety of channels for your message like newsletters, e-mail, and social media.

- Create classic, timeless brands.

CHAPTER 11

Share Feedback

A lesson I learned from crying on my first job

Fresh out of college, I was bright-eyed and ready to join the "real world." My dream at the time was to be a news reporter, so when I was offered a reporting job in my favorite city of Colorado Springs, I could barely contain my excitement.

I'll never forget my first studio session with Terry, a 60-something journalist with an impressive work history. He was incredible on the air; his voice tracks would make your ears melt! Ready to show him my best, I put on my headphones, pulled my shoulders back, leaned into the mic and read my script like a champ!

On the third sentence, Terry stopped me and started yelling about everything that was wrong with my voicing. I repeated a silent mantra to myself: "Don't cry. Don't cry. Don't cry." But trying not to cry only made me cry harder. I was embarrassed, and Terry felt horrible.

Clearly he was frustrated with my performance on air, but I didn't know how to fix it – and asking questions didn't seem to help. At the same time, I was frustrated with his aversion to using some of the newer technologies we relied upon in the studio – things that, to me, were second nature.

It took a while to figure out which direction to go, but finally we struck a deal: I would help Terry learn the technology if he'd coach me on how to do better on the air. It wasn't an overnight fix, but it was a start, and we both worked at it. He tried harder to deliver constructive criticism in a way that wouldn't make me want to run to a corner and bawl. I tried to develop a tougher skin and to talk him through the technology.

This positive change in our working relationship made a difference; before long, we had an amazing synergy that showed on the air. Having a great product – in this case a news show – only happened when we learned how to complement one another, allowing our strengths to shine while we worked together on our weaknesses.

Somewhere along the way, Terry started calling me "Princess Jess" for my once-sheltered ways, and I called him "Your Majesty" in a lighthearted deference to his vast experience and knowledge. He turned out to be one of the best mentors I've ever had.

The Bottom Line: Different generations can find working together awkward or frustrating.

The Solution: Offer consistent feedback, and be open to what you might learn by taking advantage of mentoring and reverse-mentoring opportunities. With some effort, different generations can work together for amazing outcomes.

Give feedback

When you are leading or supervising others, particularly if they're members of rising generations, it's important to provide positive and constructive feedback about how they're doing.

Keep in mind that if they're young in their experiences, they may not be sure how to baseline their efforts – and if they're used to the constant feedback loop of social media, a lack of feedback from you may be viewed as a troubling silence.

Rather than waiting for a traditional once-a-year performance review, hold informal conversations as needed – and consider setting up consistent check-in meetings to help them gauge their work and make improvements in real time.

Be clear about your intent

When giving feedback, it's important to communicate your intent. We often forget to do this part, and it can make a big difference in how the feedback is perceived. Consider this example of two different approaches:

Sally is called in for a meeting with her boss, who tells her, "I'm enrolling you in a public speaking course." She spends the rest of the day worrying because this must mean she's doing a terrible job in meetings and presentations.

Susie is called in for a meeting with her boss, who tells her, "I see a lot of potential in you, and I want to help your professional development, so I'm enrolling you in a public speaking course."

She is thrilled at the opportunity and texts her mom to say how excited she is that her boss has taken notice of her potential.

Be open to receiving feedback

So...what if the feedback you receive is not so positive? Especially if you're new on the job and enthusiastic to do well, negative feedback can be tough to swallow. But before dismissing the feedback as wrong, pause.

Take a deep breath and consider what was shared with you: Could there be some truth to it? Evaluating feedback objectively, even when it stings, is a great opportunity for personal growth and development.

Mentor and reverse-mentor

More and more the Millennial generation is involved in leading our organizations and institutions. Are you doing all you can to equip and empower them for success? Are you teaching them everything you've learned and sharing your wisdom forward?

If you've got years of knowledge and experience, then you have the opportunity to make a difference in the rising generation, one life at a time. Consider whose life you could be investing in.

At the same time, consider that mentoring is a two-way street; reverse-mentoring is learning from people who are younger than us – and we can all be inspired by their energy and optimism. I've seen CEOs learn how to tweet from 19-year old interns, and youth directors strengthen their faith because of deep questions posed by their group members.

It's OK not to have all the answers

Remember that with Millennials, it's all about relationships. Mentoring is not about having all the answers or following a specific program; it's about caring, listening, asking questions, checking in, sharing your experiences, and helping the person you're mentoring to be successful.

Mentoring can be as simple as meeting for coffee or even checking in with a text. My mentor and I both love power walking, so when we need to catch up, we hit the trail and talk it up!

CHAPTER 12

Move into the Future

"Each generation goes further than the generation preceding it because it stands on the shoulders of that generation."

– RONALD REAGAN

As we look ahead to the next decade, a major generational shift is upon us: as retiring Baby Boomers leave the workforce in droves, their children – the Millennials – are stepping into millions of jobs. Some of them are rising into leadership roles while still in their 20s.

Companies and organizations around the United States have begun to recognize the gaps in knowledge and experience that they are suddenly facing. The savvy ones have begun to look ahead with the knowledge that Baby Boomers are turning 65 at a rate of 10,000 a day[21] – and that by 2020 (less than five years from now!), Millennials will make up nearly half of the workforce.[22] They know that they have to take steps now to ensure a smooth transition and avoid knowledge loss.

While there will be the inevitable bumps in the road as this generational transition takes place, it's important to remain flexible and remember that we all have more in common than we think. Though different generations don't all take the same approach, we share many goals as we look toward the future. It's important to work together and build on our common goals to help make that future as positive as it can be.

A Challenge to Established Generations:

Thank you for the solid foundation you've laid and the knowledge you've accumulated over many years of experience.

Be intentional about passing along life lessons, traditions, knowledge, and wisdom to emerging generations – and make an effort to communicate these ideas in a way they'll understand. Whether or not they seem ready to listen, they need your knowledge and mentoring. Empower them to learn, value what they bring to the table, and live with succession in mind, preparing to help them take the reins of leadership when you're ready to step down.

A Challenge to Emerging Generations:

I know you've probably heard this before, but there really is a lot you can learn from those who've gone before you, so please take time to listen and to ask questions.

Be open to and respectful of advice from established generations, and build on that knowledge to make meaningful improvements as you work to make yourselves worthy leaders. Be willing to show respect for other experiences and listen well as you work to make this a better world for future generations; someday, you too will be passing the torch.

ReGenerate

No matter which generation you're part of, remember that sharing stories and experiences strengthens our understanding of one another and our understanding of the importance of both past and present realities in shaping who we are as people and organizations.

Though there's always potential for misunderstanding and conflict when different generations interact, there's also potential to work together in ways that result in a better outcome than any one generation could achieve on its own. So let's listen to and help one another, and put in the effort necessary to make our generational differences and strengths work together for a win-win.

Experience has proven that organizations, schools, churches, families, and communities that leverage the collective value of multiple generations will thrive time after time: they will ReGenerate.

REFERENCES

1. Karl Mannheim, "The Problem of Generations," in *From Karl Mannheim*, ed. Kurt H. Wolff, 2nd expanded edition (New Brunswick, NJ: Transaction, 1993), 365.

2. William Strauss and Neil Howe, *Generations: The History of America's Future, 1584 to 2069* (New York: Morrow, 1991).

3. "Millennials: Confident. Connected. Open to Change," Pew Research Center, accessed January 19, 2015, http://www.pewsocialtrends.org/files/2010/10/millennials-confident-connected-open-to-change.pdf.

4. Barna Group OmniPoll. Study conducted in 2014 with a representative sample of at least 1000 U.S. adults, ages 18+. Data was conducted by telephone (including with cellphone users) and online.

5. Anya Kamenetz, "The Four-Year Career," *Fast Company*, January 12, 2012.

6. "Median Household Income in the United States," DaveManuel.com, accessed January 19, 2015, http://www.davemanuel.com/median-household-income.php.

7. Les Christie, "America's Homes Are Bigger than Ever," CNNMoney, accessed January 19, 2015, http://money.cnn.com/2014/06/04/real_estate/american-home-size/.

8. Kim Parker and Eileen Patten, "The Sandwich Generation," Pew Research Center, accessed January 19, 2015, http://www.pewsocialtrends.org/2013/01/30/the-sandwich-generation/.

9. "Births, Deaths, Marriages, and Divorces," *Statistical Abstract of the United States*, U.S. Census Bureau, accessed January 19, 2015, http://www.census.gov/prod/2011pubs/11statab/vitstat.pdf.

10. "A Half-Century Of Learning: Historical Census Statistics On Educational Attainment in the United States, 1940 to 2000," US Census Bureau, accessed January 19, 2015, http://www.census.gov/hhes/socdemo/education/data/census/half-century/tables.html.

11. Sylvia Ann Hewlett, "4 Ways To Retain Gen Xers," *Harvard Business Review*, September 4, 2014.

12. Sylvia Ann Hewlett and Lauren Chivee, *The X Factor: Tapping into the Strengths of the 35- to 48-Year-Old Generation* (New York: Rare Bird, 2013).

13. "The PreparedU Project's Report on Millennial Minds," *The Millennial Mind Goes to Work*, Bentley University, accessed January 19, 2015, http://www.bentley.edu/newsroom/latest-headlines/mind-of-millennial.

14. "Millennials in Adulthood," Pew Research Center, accessed January 19, 2015, http://www.pewsocialtrends.org/2014/03/07/millennials-in-adulthood/.

15. "Millennials in Adulthood." Births: Final Data for 2012," *National Vital Statistics Reports* 62.9 (2013), Centers for Disease Control, accessed January 19, 2015, http://www.cdc.gov/nchs/data/nvsr/nvsr62/nvsr62_09.pdf. "U.S. Census Bureau Projections Show a Slower Growing, Older, More Diverse Nation a Half Century from Now," U.S. Census Bureau, accessed January 19,

2015, https://www.census.gov/newsroom/releases/archives/population/cb12-243.html.

16. "Millennials in Adulthood."

17. "Social Networking Fact Sheet,"Pew Research Center, accessed January 19, 2015, http://www.pewinternet.org/fact-sheets/social-networking-fact-sheet/.

18. "Millenials in Adulthood."

19. "Births: Final Data for 2012."

20. Andrew Kohut, "What Will Become of America's Kids?," *FactTank: News in the Numbers*, Pew Research Center, accessed January 19, 2015, http://www.pewresearch.org/fact-tank/2014/05/12/what-will-become-of-americas-kids/.

21. D'Vera Cohn and Paul Taylor, "Baby Boomers Approach 65 – Glumly," Pew Research Center, accessed January 19, 2015, http://www.pewsocialtrends.org/2010/12/20/baby-boomers-approach-65-glumly/.

22. Jessica Brack, "Maximizing Millennials in the Workplace," UNC Kenan-Flagler Business School, accessed January 19, 2015, http://www.kenan-flagler.unc.edu/executive-development/custom-programs/~/media/DF1C11C056874DDA8097271A1ED48662.ashx.

Acknowledgements

Thank you to Debra McCown for helping me translate the words from my head and heart into the pages of this book.

Thank you to René Rodgers for copy editing, Briana Morris for graphics, and Matt Haynes for cover design.

Thank you to my clients, who continue to encourage and inspire me.

Most of all, thank you to my family – Mom and Dad, Emily, Allie-Kate, Chris, Nolan and Lilly G – and to my precious friends for always sticking by my side and believing in my dreams.

For every copy of *ReGenerations* purchased, we will donate $1 to the YWCA Bristol youth programs, which are helping the next generation to empower women and eliminate racism.

To keep up with ReGenerations, please visit us online at www.re-generations.org.

You can also connect with us on Twitter, @ReGenerations, and Facebook, ReGenerations.

To book a speaking or training event, email info@regenerations.org.

Made in the USA
Charleston, SC
19 May 2015